WORDS FROM THE WALL

WORDS FROM THE WALL

Adam Thorpe

CAPE POETRY

1 3 5 7 9 10 8 6 4 2

Jonathan Cape, an imprint of Vintage,
20 Vauxhall Bridge Road,
London SW1V 2SA

Jonathan Cape is part of the Penguin Random House group of companies
whose addresses can be found at global.penguinrandomhouse.com.

First published by Jonathan Cape in 2019

penguin.co.uk/vintage

A CIP catalogue record for this book is available
from the British Library

ISBN 9781787330993

Typeset in 11/13 pt Bembo by Jouve (UK), Milton Keynes
Printed and bound in Great Britain by TJ International Ltd, Padstow, Cornwall

Penguin Random House is committed to a sustainable future for
our business, our readers and our planet. This book is made
from Forest Stewardship Council® certified paper.

In memory of John Moat

CONTENTS

WORDS FROM THE WALL

TIBERIUS TO CALIGULA

after Suetonius

Capri, 31 AD

I.

Come here, Little Boots,
sit by me. Take my hand.

Tenderness and compassion are finished.
Love is hysterical. We are naturally vicious.

Don't flinch:
my suppurating boils

are the gods' game. Likewise my breath.
Teeth, digestion. Stand on the cliffs

and watch the transit of the waves.
They are never the same. They voluntarily shatter

their glassy forms on the harshness of rock.
It is entirely natural, like our family snout.

Those appalling screams are transmitted
by a system of silver tubes

and giant amphorae – clever, clever –
positioned in the corners of the pleasure rooms,

the secret arbours in the palace grounds,
the numberless dungeons, and even

in my brand-new
prosectorium. Pain

or pleasure?
The ambiguity delights me.

Sometimes you will hear my voice.
My weary, old-fashioned voice.

Don't ask me how it works.
Even the breakers far below

the execution cliff, where those who've disobeyed
are swallowed up in a thunder

and hiss of foam, trashed to limblessness
by dear old Neptune,

do not quite smother it.
Like words in your head,

going on forever. Ad infinitum!
I am well read. Scholastically inclined.

A stern headmaster
with private cupboards full of porn!

We have twelve villas, with proper plumbing,
splendid terraces and sparkling views of the sea.

When you see a woman,
transparently clad or entirely nude

padding through the olive groves,
grab her by just anywhere you like.

They are commanded
to like it.

They like it.

2.

Little boots, do not be sad.
Your adoring uncle will be disappointed.

Let me tell you one big thing:
I never lie.

Forget Rome. Rome is over.
Forget your mother, your brothers,

they are definitely dead.
Forget the old world. Dismissed.

Defunct. Now
it is all Capri, all joy

in the perfume of pine sap,
the golden flowers of the flowering broom, etcetera.

Breathe it in. You see how the sea renews itself
at every moment? Now and now and now.

Likewise we are awash with expectation:
life is beautiful. You are beautiful.

We expect so much from you,
Little Boots, in the years to come

on our magic island, high-security, wonderful.
Wonderful, amazing things.

You are only eighteen,
but trembling is never an option. Warning!

Nor is weeping. Only slaves
and women weep.

And the beautiful children.
When Drusus died? Yes, I wept.

I cannot lie. I was terribly sad.
I was almost broken.

My sweet young brother, my own blood.
My one friend.

The black and swollen broken leg.
The careless idiot fell from his horse.

I walked back to Rome in front of his corpse.
All the way back from Germania.

I wore them out, my leather soles,
on the paved lengths, stretching to the heavens

between the shading ilex, the stripes of cypresses
and wore away my tears as well.

I dared to curse the gods, however.
Who, by the way,

do not exist.
Your sweet old uncle

is the only mortal to be granted
this horrible, horrible fact about the gods:

they told him. As real as my fist. Horrible
but true. Don't look so surprised.

Sit closer, pray.
Let me touch your face.

Everything is rumour. Don't
believe a word of what they say.

UNBURIED

for Simon Dormandy

Up under the roof-joists of that vast, abandoned church
we'd borrowed for our arcane drama-performance research

we found a cat's skeleton, perfectly curled on a pouffe
of its own dust. Nothing had stirred it for years, aloof

above the throng . . . maybe for decades. It felt so alone.
Had crept aloft one day, dragging its rear, not a moan

or a whimper (as cats in great pain keep it quiet
for fear of the predator), and lay down out of sight

and died where no one came. You'd have thought the rats . . .
but no: it subsided to dust out of water and muscle and fats

undisturbed. There was constancy in it, a kind of faith.
Its world of timbers smelt faintly of smoke, a wraith

from Victorian or even Georgian London, all must
and dry rot. The cat was its own installation, its dust

sculpted by nothing but gravity, flush with the floor's
rough planks in a cartoon splat of dessicated gore,

no earth to be absorbed by, and even the fur had flown.
But cats are particularly frightening when reduced to bone:

spindly-limbed, dinosaur-toothed, with huge voids
where the eyes once were, the curved spine reptiloid

with tiny hips, or like a pike's on a finished plate. One
still stops me entering the backmost part of our barn:

picked out in torchlight by chance, it visually screeched
from the littered straw. A cat, that's all! It'll hardly scratch.

More decades on, I guess it won't have just disappeared.
Stripped down in the interim to some essential fear,

its unsound sleep is not like that peaceful London find:
boggle-eyed in that lightless room like the back of my mind,

it rolls and paws and twitches its ears, restless as a lie,
waiting for my scuttle of life to dare to enter and die.

THE ALARM

Sounds better in French, *insomnie*,
its whisper of sleeplessness, light-footedly
summoning you to stay . . .
You stare out each worry, aghast
at their number. Admit you can die.

On the glossier edges of your life
you learn in braille
the hundred-odd basic postures
of Indian dance. This, like everything else,
is a waste of time: the new day

with its pennants fluttering
spreads on the horizon
while you're running for a plane
that touched down earlier
than you'd anticipated, a puff of rubber.

And then you drift out of sight
to yourself, your dreams unspooled
to the calm of night-time airports
and half-familiar faces on the sacred mound
with an ambient mosquito buzz

growing like a gryke from a limestone cliff
until a hand is too small to flatten it
and your entire body is urgently required
to climb up there in cuisse, vambrace, a clatter of plackart
and hurl yourself into the game again.

TREBARWITH

i.m. Robert Avery

Hail skittering off stone and skin, our
brave face on it (down beyond the hood

to nose and chin) getting it
just as much as that slab, tufted by thrift

but unstirred. The majestic variables
of the weather, here: it was sunlight

and warmth a few moments ago!
Though we tighten our draw-cords

to a crackle and fizz of impermeables,
we can still hear the breakers beyond the edge,

their quarrelling over the cliffs
a long way down, working into hairline

cracks or chasms you could star-jump in,
a flawless geology of faults taken

advantage of by this ceaselessness, like the verge
of breakdown. Look, the rock's toothed racks

are meshed with foam, as if the whole
machinery of the coast might one day

cough into motion, inch by inch, its line
advancing on the map towards the crease of fold,

the world flapping and completely uncontrollable.

AGINCOURT

1. *Dysentery*

Dad came home to Calcutta
from a three-day work-trip to Katmandu
to find my mother all but dead.

A desiccated husk in a near coma.
I didn't know; doubtless kept asking my *ayah*.
Mum lived, of course, but then went blind

from the wonder drug being India-trialled
by the Japanese. She wouldn't have been able to see
this field, these trees, the ooze at our feet

at fifty-eight, as I am now.
'I'd never felt so ghastly in all my life!'
Yet here they stood, the archers, in their own

ghastliness, sodden and soiled, the death-stench
misting at their mouths, and went on pulling
against the draw-weight of a blindness that lasts forever.

2. *Malcolm, 1918*

'One of the war's greatest triumphs'
General Sir Arthur Currie

An hour east of Agincourt, off the Arras-Cambrai road,
my great-uncle Malcolm, aged twenty-seven, handsome
in the dress of a Seaforth Highlander, bare-kneed

in his kilt, floundered through chopped-up clart, the same
slippery Somme kind as the knights here charged in steel.
Advancing at dawn through September drizzle, towards

a low ridge sparkling with machine-guns, its shells
splattering the lines and drowning the piper's skreel,
at some point that morning he faltered and fell.

Laid to rest in that same ground, soon grassed
and walled like a garden, to where I have also
floundered in boots made big by this clay –

crouching to his tomb, saying his name through tears –
he's always behaved as if we were close, as though
our two lives overlapped and I must love him, too.

3. Henry's Tomb

The Abbey's keeper of collections has allowed us so near,
up in the roped-off Confessor's Chapel, stepping out
onto the very plinth, that I can stroke the effigy

of bare oak blackened by age (the gilt long stolen)
and hear his voice (Olivier's, mostly). The glittering legend
is now mere bones, a skull with a drilled cheek

where the arrow's point at Shrewsbury lodged. His friends
were few: the Bishop of Norwich lies like a lover
beneath this tomb, with a ruby ring. Avoiding women,

the king was pious, aloof: the type of boss
who'd not even look at you in the corridor, whose visions
were so vast they stretched to the walls of Jerusalem.

He was also good on detail, like God – Whose will
was his own, of course: he ordered the soldier hanged
who'd stolen a little nothing from a church; personally stocked

the campaign to the last horseshoe. Remarkably brave, too.
Evensong begins as we gaze, as lovely as England.
You see what I mean? We are all in his head, his head

is everything: this Abbey he endowed to completion,
Shakespeare, God, mud. The screams of the dying.
Our BBC microphone with its fluffy hood. The black heartwood.

4. *Ghosts*

On misty dawns they're seen, blackened
up to their chins, a rugby team
of burly thousands, slowly moving forward

as if to some final decision, some
explanatory crest. The living have left:
these are the ones who were lost

in that spasm of a field's slow time,
wraiths risen from the ploughland,
brushing the sugar beet in cold October

or a brief stir of breeze in the man-size maize.
Shall we join them? Shoulder to shoulder
with the cold dead, loose-bowelled with fear,

meeting the forged and sharpened hail
that makes not a sound as it falls
from the sky's flatlands, will we become,

at the very end, almost courageous too?

5. *Game*

On a vasty pitch of puddled chalkland,
peering out on the world
through our tin colanders,
we are boys once more in a game

where the girls are forbidden
even to watch from the edge:
they'd seem too real, turning
our treble yells and bare-kneed charge

into giggles and farce. The weaker
agree to survive intact, while the stronger
elect themselves to moan and writhe
from horrible wounds, as they always do.

COMMUTERS

We're in a rut, we say, as if life's
a laden cart and not a car –
small, hired – stuck behind a truck
on the M25 at rush hour
in, say, fog. So certain phrases

trundle on at their own pace,
cheerily waving as everything else
whips past them. A kind of debris.
For the two men in this early train,
in grey suits and polished shoes, worrying

away at their laptops and smartphones
as they're belted far from Basingstoke
and their dawn-tinged homes, the issue (well,
according to the hard-pressed one with specs)
is as above: *We're in a rut*.

And immediately I see leather-clad peasants
floundering in ooze, rain falling,
the half-starved nag stubborn under the whip –
not the draft interim statement
spread on the table between us,

my coffee shivering at the sheer speed.

CHINOOKS

They would press their ears hard to the ground
'for the warning', she says: bright-eyed behind
black-rimmed glasses, essaying her English.

Her grandfather's generation, now: he fought
for the Vietcong. For the Revolution!
So whenever the Americans came

the villagers were hiding 'in the earth', below.
She's staring out at the glassy breakers
with their scrolled-back foam, gunmetal grey

beneath a clouded sky. 'You've read of China
wanting our sea?' 'Of course.' 'Why can't we
Vietnamese just be keeping what is ours,

our sea, our land?' I babble something about
global strategy, the schemes, the scrabbles
of history as the balmy, tropical air blows in,

indifferent either way. 'I suppose rotors
are very loud,' I conjecture, and mime
the twirl of the blades. 'They couldn't *hear*,' she says,

'they were too far away!' (The vibrations, stupid.)
'They *sensed* it,' I suggest. 'They sensed it
through the ground.' Like a distant train

singing in the rails. She nods. The conical hats
were bobbing about in the paddy fields as they always
will, the Chinooks like grotesque insects looming

over the hills too late to operate
their deadly chatter. What will it take for people
to bend down to the ground and hear? No,

not hear, for as she said it wasn't the whumps
of the rotors that alerted them, but the motion
in the air, the vibrations, the shift and knock

of the pressured soil, the fluid molecules,
the belonging to her people of the broken land.
Its hurt, its crying out, *Beware, beware,*

the Chinooks are on their way! We wouldn't have
a clue what was coming, now . . . deaf to the earth
and upright as we are, our hands brushed clean

of saving soil, and the wind already turned.

HUSH

1.

Only the loud squeak of the heavy-doored
phone box bang in front, its muffled tender
of chat and goster, an occasional episode of shrieks.

Contemplative cottage, where I'd tilt
at something grand like *Don Quixote*
or scribble verse upstairs in thick socks

as you knitted that jumper over Plath's *Letters*.
A timpani of leaks from the bucket,
the coal fire's sour coughs thickened

by certain winds off the moors. A familiarity
of damp and Vim, the *GEC* fridge humming and hawing.
Volcanic outcrops pocked like sponges beyond the back yard.

2.

My father left the village at sixteen. The war!
God, what must that mean, to be born and bred
in the same place? He'd raised his hand

when the colonel came in '41, college
swapped for a uniform, the deaths of friends, 'freedom
abroad'. The locals like Eric who'd known him:

stories I'd record over hours on cassette,
stomping the heavy buttons home.
'Just a sec. Record.' Tales from the Peaks! 'He were

away a bit, our Bernard, but now he's back.' Over
thirty years, Eric! 'Ey up, you forget.
Feels like ten . . .' Laughing, then off

down Main Street, limping from the attack
on the aerodrome, shrapnel still in.
Time varies for no one. Not Eric, not Dad.

Although there's nowhere for me to be
away from like them,
another thirty's gone since then.

BATACLAN

in memoriam 13/11/2015

Everything to hope for
in their homely scarves, their ingenuous smiles

for the archive snapshots –
as if they have drifted without alarm or soared

into flight from wherever they were harboured
in affection's sea light, secured by all those

blameless ropes we know nothing about
and would never have conceived of

if we'd passed them unsmiling
in the street: all those future angels,

all those stations of flame.

UNPERSON

My chance companion on the organised hike
has the build of a stork, though nudging seventy.

He sounds familiar, weirdly, like the voice
of the stranger on the road to Emmaus –

posher, of course, than the ghost of the son
of a carpenter, though not much less sepulchral;

it is sending beeps through the fog of memory,
anyway, as we skirt the sluther of a Suffolk field

shoulder to shoulder, making conversation.
It's almost creepy. Anterior, or an inner

conscience I should have listened to.
An actor, of course. Worming his way in

through a children's series from the sixties,
long forgotten. Or maybe I've known him

in a dream, or some parallel life
broken away from. No, he was never an actor.

Nor a teacher: mine, or anyone's. He takes
a breath. 'Announcer for Radio 3, retired.

Actually, given the push. Not smiling enough!
But great music is a serious matter,' he goes on,

through the oceanic hiss of the Scots pines.
'Well, you can *hear* smiles, you see.

Or so they claimed. And now it's all
grins and natter. Classics in small lumps.'

The intimate soothe of his background gloss
fled from the wireless, it walks beside me

in heavy boots, the squelch of their tread
like sound effects. 'I was abolished,' he continues.

'An unperson, to use Orwell's term. Yesterday's model.
Untimely ripped,' he adds, with a hollow chuckle.

Mendelssohn. Chopin's Mazurka in C sharp minor.
Telemann, Britten, Bach. A talk on Wilde.

The long, serious silence of Cage.
I tell him how I miss his voice, even

after all these years: lying in bed
or cross-ankled in front of the grate,

struggling with an essay or a poem.
Spreading toast. Doing nothing. Life

in England, before everything went
for hire or askew. As if talking,

I realise, to someone close I've known
since childhood, who's now deceased.

Then, abruptly halting on the path
with a smile, his old-fashioned actor's *R*

like a tapped valve, the timbre soft
as peach fur, leaning towards me

as if over its own coffin: 'It never
occurred to me, you know.

That I might be missed.'

BEACHED

Snæfellsnes Peninsula, Iceland

1.

A handmade sign on the road: *Dead Whale Here*
as if for sale, like clams; then a long dirt track
between fistfuls of grass, salt marsh, the odd lagoon.

A hint of uncured fish left out too long.
Then a gust of something even fouler
than the usual blench of sulphurous gas

as we abandon the car where the ground's
too soft and head for the ridge of shingle
screening the beach. From up on top,

seen across the black and bouldery stretch
of laval foreshore, it's just a well-stuffed sock;
but crunching closer, slipping on algal drift-heaps

swarmed by gnats, we watch it grow
to a refugee's bodybag, stretched to unbearable size.
No one claims it. No one wants to know.

2.

Four months on from when this airship's calm
juddered into gravity and the local newsboard
displayed the corpse intact, still glossed, it's more

24

a magnified flop of bladderwrack than lovely
cetacean, than singing cachalot.
'Beached whale' vies in my head with *hvalreki*

which means 'windfall' as well: the ocean's legacy,
the fruit blown down. So lean were the turf-roofed days
that when the sea gave freely to a land

stripped of its forests by the Norse
it was a stroke of luck. Near it sprawls a carcass
gingery with rust – part of a wartime hull

or merchantman's keel ripped from its berth in a storm,
as free of foulness as it was of breath:
now it's been joined by something even the gulls

avoid – that bleeds a petrol of ambergris
from the seaward flank where the waves are forcing a kyle
and the tide has that coppery, urotoxic tint

of the freighter's bilge, the factory's run-off,
the slime of Sellafield. It'll all be tidied
by worms come winter: a ribbed vault of baleen

bleached by spindrift. That curious, roving eye
is now a square, chopped free for a souvenir
and blind as a skylight. Others have spired

sea-smoothed pebbles on the bluff of brow
or sawn off the lower jaw for the biddable teeth
or dented the old truck's bonnet of a snout

that gives no hint of the depths it graced, their extreme
pressure. Here is the biggest brain on the planet.
I'd write a sonnet were it not for the stench.

3.

Drop by drop, like age, rot titrates:
the blow-hole down one side's now sunk to a crater,
though the tiny flaps (vestigial legs

once running like a deer's) lend a note of feeling –
pathos, even – to this open dump's
lack of discretion; and no one's even bothered

to steal the giant lamprey of cock draped
down the side, as long as a person. This
is all of us coming to grief: sudden or slow,

bubbling to a slop, we'll stop. Like this.
Beating a retreat, at last, to where you're perched
on a rock in an upwind sunspot

I hold your hand, inhale the landscape like mint.
The pure relief of mountain upon mountain;
Greenland concealed by a glitter of ocean;

the waiting volcano of Snæfellsjökull, its snow
whitecap still holding on. A williwaw
gust, straight off the peaks, cuts to the bone

and stirs your hair to tickle my cheek . . . companionship's
purchase on love's fresh air, our windfalls bouncing
somewhere, we hope, on all those lawns to come.

HOPING

Hoping the end will be swift, not as slow
as my mother's, say, who joked

almost to the end; broken neck in a brace
for months, blind, trapped in Basingstoke's

sore hell of a hospital, the patient care
minimal, the tea always cold. Her face

was Hamm's behind the shades, but her jokes
were Clov's: 'Things are livening up . . .'

'What on earth is there to keep me here?'
A whisky soda on ice was what she craved,

and last of all not love but a comb
of her hair, 'when push comes to shove',

and her metal nail-file that she laid
in her palm like a lifeline, gazing

down on it for nearly an hour.

CONFERENCE

Wannsee, Berlin

Up in my own room, gratefully alone,
I hit and rehit my back space key

like a crazy jazz pianist repeating the one note
until the whole poem's swallowed up

in white. That's the way. Swans asleep
against snow, broken kaleidoscope.

The final day is earnest, head down in words,
then it's everyone up to the frozen lake

which talks like a trapped walrus pack –
those groans from underground. Is ice

ground, in fact? We're not quite sure of this
but walk out on its soluble crust

nevertheless – apparent authors of our own destiny,
hallooing each other in the freeze: *horror vacui*.

Near the locked-in concrete bridge
with its stoic *glasnost* graffiti

we watch a pair of skaters weave
such smooth rings around all the questions

we've posed so cautiously in our unsuitable shoes
in the huge and overheated conference room . . .

Blunt nibs. We've not progressed one inch,
it seems to me. Intolerable to admit, however:

the ice under us squeaky as a door,
our breath collecting lustrous on the scarves

as we promise to keep in touch.
Hugging and laughing in a cloud of fibs.

EDGE

The Strandir coast begins with a dirt track,
the guttural end of tarmac in a waste

of bared rock, grass and scree,
and empty coves where great white trunks

have floated from Siberia: they litter
the vast and stony strands

like matches if seen from afar, but down
among them now they block our way

in booms of perimeter barriers,
logs pale as the long drowned,

stripped of bark to the white of washed-up
sea-tangle, unburied thigh-bones.

Some have mortises in them, like masts
ripped of their tenons from a stricken fleet;

all are dead straight, glittering with salt,
rubbed smooth like something someone

wishes to be lovely. I don't quite understand.
Are they overspill from Russian lumber yards,

or the tide's natural kill, taken out of trade
and odyssey? Or a sign, possibly,

of some deeper injury, like precocious
ice-melt? Up here in the north

of Iceland, anyway, it all seems clear:
the land is flat, tufted by grass and thrift,

buttressed by the odd outcrop, and stretches
bare of trees to the horizon, which is always

the sea . . . no houses, cars, wires or people
except for us two, feeling as though

we've finally come to some
personal typology, some intimate edge

and that we're almost at the start
once more, shivering in mid-summer cold,

locked-on for good to a second life
where all we do is stride through sedge

and smell what we can eat on the wind.

FIT FOR PURPOSE

Bolzano, Italy

At times I confess that my parents' old joke
about their eldest being 'a mistake' (they'd been married
a matter of weeks, wanted to be free
for longer), has more significance
than they'd intended. The heart

has never been in it, quite,
finding that so much irritates,
is alien. Not just that American, sugary,
automated computer voice telling me
my *virus database has been updated*,

but the whole wash of it
spinning in my head. I'm not
quite fit for purpose, as is said
by those who are. Did the Ice Man
ever think this? Looking at his knots

where thought nestles like a bird,
I see no doubt, no irritation. Pain,
perhaps, from whipworm, quern-savaged
teeth, his Lyme's. He knew how
everything he had fashioned worked,

but nature was a mystery. The vault
of stars: what did he see in them?
Everything but what they are – burning
plasma, thermonuclear fusion, impossibly
far. What stories did they spin, for him?

We have no idea, but his ideas were good
enough to walk with, see his way by, living
so light he could carry his own survival,
belt and backpack, quiver, pouch.
His clothes stitched from animal skin

so he is part animal, stinking of pelt
and hide. Yes, he fitted in – much
better than we are in our unidirectional
Now, though we know how to weave,
surf the web, or why stars burn.

The reign of the measure. Wind-speed.
The molecular properties of snow.
Where the oil is buried, or the coal.
Preferring the plumbline of purpose, not cartilage
tattooed into health again, nor a cap

patched from bear fur so that bear
is in you, nor a straw dryness in your shoe.
All these we can do without, now that
every knot's undone – and thought with them.
What is there to fear? That the path

leads nowhere as we stumble on?
Looking through the porthole
into the refrigerated cell, I see
the gleaming body in its sleeve of ice
not as perpetuity but as sheer chance,

the five-thousand-three-hundred-years-ago throw
of some cosmic dice that meant he would die
just where the snow could caul him tight
to thaw on the day those two chance hikers
(abandoning the path!) would be there to spot him.

And whose mistake was that one?

IT WAS COLDER THEN

I.

My bedroom window would be varicose
with frost, though the bed was warm: a quick
lick-and-promise flannel, Weetabix, teeth,

then out in regulation shorts and cardi –
as if my form, while enormous to itself,
was too small for the air to notice

on its non-stop flight from the Urals.
Or maybe we were thicker-skinned, like the cars:
our little Simca would usually start

in a swirl of choke, ticking over
as the windscreen was rediscovered
under the tough-guy attack of the scraper

or succumbed to water safely off the boil
in a mushroom cloud of steam I'd stand in,
pretending to die, thorax already sore.

It was the salt-spreader that made us
late one time, my father cursing
what the 'muck' would do to the underside,

to the nooks and crannies: the rust
'that never sleeps', like radiation, or whatever
was working on my mother's eyes.

One suede glove hovering on the gear-stick,
its Injun mate would gallop on the wheel
as we inched forward in our miniature

submarine through the depths of the morning:
he towards a nightmare day of ice at Heathrow,
me towards the dread of being late for assembly –

stepping in like Tintin into the Temple of the Sun
with the whole knelt-down school turning towards me
as one angelic face facing mine – tainted and aflame.

2.

It was colder then. On the way to the farm
the deeper ruts showed skylights
my Tuf shoes (animal prints on the rubber soles:
stag, fox, badger, stoat) would merely creak

and twang, however hard I smote.
The working compass secreted in the heel
soon broken, the raised prints stubbed already
from recognition, I would never track,

like one of the Cheyenne, hedgehog,
otter, red squirrel or goat: only
a sheep in occasional snow, the indistinction
of hooves in mud, the penitentiary

cartoon pattern of birds on builders' sand.

MUD PUDDLE

I.

There is thought down there, or even
conjecture. An appetite like a famished pike's.

My grandfather's *Classical Myth and Legend*
would fall open to Hylas, as painted by Waterhouse,

still among the living on the water's edge,
precariously leaning with his shiny jug

towards a pubescent flotilla of girls,
their long hair dark as the pond's sludge.

He was me, baffled at the age of twelve.
Nipple-deprived, albino-white, with succulent,

vermilion lips, it was only their desire
that made them desirable. I wanted to be

lord of the underwater gloam, spoilt silly,
wrapped in their waist-length russet hair

like the clammy entanglements of *Myriophyllum
spicatum*, laughing open-mouthed without

the bubbles of air. A treasured trophy,
concealed from my family under lily-pads.

2.

The summer has been dry: already the levels
are descending, the inlets showing their ribbed

banks, like a tyre's treads. At my next school
there is to be a legendary place –

a high-roofed skylight over the girls' showers
that some will crawl to, always

disappointed by the fogs of steam,
that blur of condensation as the hot pipes

ring beneath them, voyeur-defying. It will
always be like this, with nothing to see

bar one's own face, like an ugly Narcissus
dreaming of nymphs: devising that other myth.

EMISSIONS

They're usually measured like a rising fever
from 1970, the year I first boarded, the year
I became unhappy as a sort of background

hum, the shadowy brown tone of a Chardin.
From the summer on, at least; up until then
I was only sad in bursts – when our dog

was killed by a car, or when I waited for hours
to be picked up after school by Richard's mum
who had fallen over on the ice and died

that afternoon. But my sadness emissions
first went up dramatically that year,
according to the appropriate graphs,

like a PSA spike that says: *uh-oh*.
I had to read *Lord of the Flies*, recognised
Jack's savages in most of those around me,

life as a staked and fly-blown sow's head
and the dorms as islands with monsters
for nightmares, or vice-versa. The others

had been boarders for years, toughened
in an absence of mothers. They knew the drill.
I was soft as marshmallows, and when

caught pillow-fighting and thrashed by Mr Dane
or suddenly needing glasses, I almost cried.
Then Timothy died on an Outdoor Activities

trip to Snowdonia: there were jokes and giggles.
They seemed insane, but now I think that
in my unshared shock and grief

I failed to see how thin the ice was
on which they strode, that if only
one of us in assembly had begun to sob

the whole lot there would have joined in.
Or maybe not. Maybe he'd have been jeered at,
or left out on the flat roof all night in the rain

'to study the stars' again; to become a man.

2.

Alone in the vast ward of the school
sanatorium at the beginning of term,
faking 'flu by dipping the nurse's thermometer

into a mug of tea, crash-landed in the 'sanny'
where boys had died of sore throats once,
in imagined droves, in those very iron beds,

my despair rose to a dangerous degree.
I'd learnt who was really in charge,
how frail and insufficient a thing

is kindness, or charity, or love: a mere tinge
against the walloping, brash splash
of looking-after-number-one, of the bully

who hugs you against his chest to squeeze
the living daylights out of your heart –
unsufferable shame, not pain, because

you won't ever stop him, no matter what.
The iron beds stretch out one by one
and even the bleached corridors are empty.

And when the glum nurse comes, tapping in
on strangely impractical high heels,
you're on your own, waving your thermometer,

the 1950s *Punch* sliding from your knees
like the contraband of laughter smuggled in
from before you were born, when everything was better.

CONFESSION

Douala, Cameroon

Me and Chris, in Africa
(white boys both, our voices freshly broken),

shot at the pool's incumbent frogs
with a Webley rifle belonging to his father.

Yeah, it was cool
when they exploded:

white stuff spreading like semen
through the greenish haze.

The tiny corpses, bewildered,
floated around like kids

in rubber rings of shattered flesh.
Little-boys-lost, fumbling through our teens,

we couldn't be content
with larking about on a lilo,

with somersaulting in.
It never occurred to us

that the pinched-waist pellets
might choke the filter.

We were insouciant: poachers without a keeper.
And we had all day, its steamed air ours

to make virile with a pause
for iced Fanta, legs set apart, all swagger,

the lawn's mandibles biting our feet;
cackling over old numbers of *Men Only*

that took the humidity like any
mechanism there – badly.

What was Africa to me
but having fun? The survivors kicked

and fled as we swam,
the unlucky insects pinned to the top

like ragged specimens of waste silk.
We justified our slaughter, however:

cleaning the area of pests,
mopping up, we were almost adult

in the zeal we applied to the job in hand
with a system more efficient than nets.

Time-saving! Profitable!
We were shits.

I say sorry to the frogs, every one.
Underlying each life we took

was its own spawn lost
from the brackish places

between the roots of mangroves
or in the rivers' shallows among hippos,

crocs, the not unmoral gorillas:
all humming along quite pleasantly

until we hit town . . .
a couple of Jack Ketches

who kicked away the ladder
and laughed

like everyone in the world
as the whole lot swung.

EFFET CÉVENOL

A path in spate – sudden stream conversion –
our back door facing a water curtain
like a studio set, some technician overdoing it overhead
for television, except that it's real.

I can't stand it when our neighbour, the psychotic hunter,
does something that turns the boar's grunts
to human screams of slaughter
and hope our French monsoon will fetch away

his sheds, his oven, his massive freezer rumbling
its warning. But water doesn't judge, it just comes
in a rush, leaving a sludge behind it
full of cars and trees, the homes sheared

from all the dinners that were ever eaten,
from all foundations. Whenever solidity is beaten
by flood, the fields of maize or vines look shat on.
The water edges over our back-door sill,

fattens into a pool we mop and moan about
as people do on the news who've lost the lot.
Our garden's acquired a trench where my duct
for the torrent was insufficient, was roiled out

and the rocks with it. A speed typist on the skylight.
Half a year of Paris's rainfall in one night!
Dawn comes white and calm as sea-fog, like hospital
curtains drawn tight around the mess, its slime

toyed with by sleepless surgeons who've now left.

LINGUA FRANCA

This soft wax of language, history-impressed.
The frost and fog of Danelaw, its oafs and their knives
staggered from; the Saxon hog snuffling in its barn,
dung-daggled, furrowing through acorns
in the winter wood. And ice, yonder.

Then the dainty slices of beef and monarchy,
the poor in the ditch along with the *atheling*,
favourite boys growing to military age,
the jangle of chain mail.
Owndom to property. *Wild* to savage.

Every time we open our mouths
it rushes out in a skein of colour:
entwined ghosts. Blistered with use, crying
to be recognised, the past avails us of its burden
syllable by syllable.

I write it all down like a blithe scrivener
as the slaughterers pound up the sand
from their ships, scarcely heard
over the surf's white noise, my lucidity
helpless as the scratching of mice.

STUFF

I tell my students
now here's a word that's useful:
'stuff'. *Les trucs, les choses.*

The French are too organised
to need the precise equivalent. *L'étoffe*
is mostly cloth, rubbed between the fingers.

The right stuff. Stuff happens!
Our house is full of stuff.
Did you bring the stuff ?

They warm to the theme.
I'm adding more to their brains.
Our skulls are crammed to the brim,

stuffed with the straw of facts
and memories. 'We are such stuff
as dreams are made on,' I quote.

Excrescences. Too much, too much.
Blow the dust off what's stored,
find more stuff down the sides of cupboards,

in the backs of drawers. Lose stuff.
But more accumulates. Cables
that connect nothing to nothing,

state-of-the-art stuff
no one uses any more, redundant
technology sold to us as 'cutting edge,

everyone has it', now bewildered
by the tiredness of old age.
Into the box with it, carry it off.

This was the pith of your life,
at one time. I would like a hut
of bamboo with nothing inside

save a hearth, some hens, the breeze
blowing through. That
would be enough. A cooking pot.

And the only stuff on the shelves
a heap of corn cobs,
drying in the smoke.

THE SPRAYERS

Churchyard bonfires of carvings in oak or limewood,
only slightly wormed; the punching out
of ancient stained glass invisibly pitted by weather;
almond-eyed angels with spread wings on a skim of limewash
blotched back to whiteness, along with the crowded Dooms;
the congenial, local faces of sculpted saints
made noseless as lepers, or annulled
completely by the blacksmith's hammer,
a few rasped to a smooth carapace
by the real obsessives . . .

here's looking at you, my England.
Sprayers nodding on long booms
through my childhood and my adulthood,
the meadows silenced of their quivering lyra,
the tiny throats bunged with whiffs
of cancer and formaldehyde,
the end of wake-robin, corn buttercup,
weasel's snout. The meadows themselves
taken umbrage to, ploughed under
and purified, but over and over again

by that new priesthood,
                    their chemical sacerdotage.

THE MONSTER

*Nothing is so painful to the human mind as a
great and sudden change.*
Mary Shelley

I.

My master-surgeon has drawn hieroglyphs
over my flesh, marks of the arcane:
one long ladder, five sets of dots in a square.
But why did he leave me nerves
if they can only thrill to pain?

I will stagger from here like a corpse
trailing bags of glory, drips
that feed me with awareness
of my cobbled-together state.
His minions bathe my wrinkled lips –

yet another incision. All is wound,
my brain still swirling with formaldehyde
so my dreams struggle to be heard,
as unfamiliar as these very words in my alien
room of a mind. I'm bound and bed-tied,

I'm told, for my own good; I cannot disavow
the master who has patched me into life,
who has sliced and joined and stitched me
free from darkness. I am my own
candle, like a fallen angel. I need a wife.

The mirror shows me as pale and wretched,
bowed as if old. But I am a newborn,
naked on the bed as they wash me,
the four of them giggling at something that lies
like an extra thumb stripped of its nail, forlorn

on my shaven groin, that I know
from my borrowed memories will swell
and do such things as shall terrify
in its towering completeness, stabbing
and goring until all is well.

2.

There is a sweetness at the back of my old mind,
like a walk-in larder unlatched to a nest of mice,

cake in dented tins, the helpful suggestions of cinnamon;
the new brain has the frenzied blindness

of a nettled wood at night, of stumping through it
as best one might. The hidden roots, the drifts of leaf-fall.

Never any knowing it. Hope rewired to itself
because there's nothing else: such sparks of illusion!

That my body cares for me, will be on the look-out.
The fizz where blood should be, and the clawed owl

of confusion, its sudden swoop
through the gnarl and twist of neurons.

The girls I laughed with once
in the baths' atrium
are withered and wattle-necked.
I love them still from this safe distance
through the fog, the heather's soak,
the raucous chirr of rooks . . .
the slip and slop of the appalling roads.

★

Dawn, yesterday.
Out of the blur's half-light
and his own breath
the sentry loomed. It takes more than woad
thumbed on the forehead
to make you a Pict, I quipped,
not detecting from that distance
it was merely a smear of his own gut,
sliced like a fish. As young
as I am old, tottering towards me,
he'd nothing to report but his own death.

★

The sheepish slink of a wild cat
in the shadow of a turret.
I won't name it, nor feed it chitterlings.
The barbarians smoke them on spits
over smouldering nests of heather,
absorb their souls, break our morale
with feline, fur-stripped grace:
flesh glimmering bare in acorn brown,

waxed by the winds alone, by these godawful gales
sharp as claws with sleet.
Catmen, then. Dullards with slim,
intelligent bodies. Now there's a thing.

*

We sacrifice toads, sizzle the kidneys of goats,
descry our graves in eviscerated crows.
My dearest soul, the honest truth:
I haven't the foggiest what we are doing here,
scraping invitations on birchbark,
pleading for supplies, enumerating minor woes.
From the very limit of the world,
Flavius sends you greetings, my lord.

*

I love my men. Messmates for an evening,
we compose amusing ditties,
wry obscenities around the hearth's glare.
Fruitless as a phalanx of stones
strung along the ups and downs of moorland
beneath the harpy screams of summer curlews
or winter gulls
to sea-marsh and bog-clutch at either end,
we are a mortal span
studying the spear in its own ribs.

*

When they charge now and again,
larruping and whooping out of the mist,
their hard-ons precede them
like a child's forearm and fist

53

scarlet with woodland berries,
or like an undigested scrap
from their toddlers' feasts.
When we hang them by the dozens
their cocks remain depleted, subside
into rose-hips, acorns, figs.
This is not the case
with any other terrorist.

★

The soul's ink is always wet,
leaves its shadow on the folded leaf.
I live its life out on slivers of larch,
itemising our leather requirements,
the lamentable state of the roads;
obeisance, arse-licking, countermanding daftness.
Birthday invitations mingle with regrets,
sympathy for the deaths of distant relatives,
for a fine boy freshly arrived from Rome
carved by the cold
to nothing but a cough. Pity him.
Unfit for service. Fit only for the Styx,
that dead-flat plain of asphodels.

★

Love-words would do me fine
if I dared, poetic musings
flowing like spunk from the iron nib.
Instead, as now, an urgent cargo of leather hides
'delayed for days at Catterick',
the mules sunk up to their hocks
in the black and sucking type of mud
they have out here

that reminds me, uneasily, after all these years,
of those spectral bogs in the jungles of the Ardennes.

★

Things in order. Spick and span. Eerily quiet.
No fervour, no insurrection
so far this year. Only the cold. One
out of ten, medically unavailable for duty.
Inflammation of the eyes
blurs us in droves: *lippientes*
or simple weeping for home.
Interim strength report is satisfactory.
A new supplier of dressed stone.
The sweet and heady stench
in all our quarters: these stratas of moss,
bracken and straw — spongy, rotting, warm,
swallowing everything from rings to combs
and our calloused feet to the ankle-bone.
It fills us with a sense of home.

★

Frost. Glassing the clay
heaped for our wattle fences
or freezing our arses to the toilet bench.
What I love is the sharp flash of it
after the bath-house; the apple-crunch of snow;
the hearty pummel of the gusts, like a friend
you've got pissed with slapping your back.
A sense of togetherness. My fine auxiliaries.
My wife and children, of course.
The buffer zone! Pacts with the tribes.
Pax, itself. Civilisation.
Fifty oysters from the great brown estuary.

Five thousand modii of dry cereal
for the diminishing granary.
A squeaky-new pair of *Sattuo* sandals.
All the unheralded virtues of boredom.

★

The forest is a distant shadow
visible on crests beyond the crags,
the land cleared in between
to scrub and friendly villages
where no one cuts off your legs
and the thatch smokes
and the cocks screech between the pigs
just as they would in the sunny Apennines.
The quiet holds well
bar low-flying sorties of geese.
Bar the odd bundle of terrorists
bursting from the pegged-down tarp
in a peasant wagon,
suicidal, exploding in spears and blades,
the gateway soon slippery with intestines
pointlessly released. One
we caught before he could die:
released from the weight of his bollocks,
he was thrown into the sewer
to bob about among his enemy's turds,
still spluttering about the *occupation,*
about the *invalidity of foreign invasion*
(in so many unrepeatable words).

★

Fomenting the end of order, of decency, of rule.
Native declensions infecting
everything we are used to: fleas in a favourite blanket.
Strutting on the crags, glimpsed between trees
from sandal-padded paths, by the snaking
ways of reconnaissance
when who is stalking who
is a mute question. Sneaky cat shadows.
My whispering patrols plunging into traps,
yanked up in nets. Irrepealable, trumped
by a bad hand,
now answering to no one. Discovered
eventually as a nest of bone,
green and furry with moss already,
soft as Venus's immortal fanny.

★

I still send them out
at the first sign of unrest. *Fetch your kit.*
That lovely sound of tramping feet,
sufficiently in step. The gorgeous clink and squeak
of overlapping plates and fresh leather.
Youngsters, some of them, barely tufted
at the groin. The mountains loom
in blue shadows. Reports
can be wrong. How to trust
anyone but the gods, as fickle
themselves as a tarn's ice?
Lime mortar holds well, much better than breath.
The wall is like words locked together
into one long phrase that says, over and over
through the impartial rain,
KEEP OUT. Or, if you prefer,

in shout after shout:
COME HERE AND LICK MY COCK,
BRITTUNCULI. Meanwhile,
our soldiers carve their loves
into the accommodating sandstone.
Deepening the ditch where the ground is soft,
we leave the rest to its rock. Stake out thorns.
You can't fix everything all the time.
Turf, stacked high, stretches it further.
So we stare from our imperial *limes*
like painted figures out of a plaster wall,
held in by artifice, characters in a dream
we hope we'll not be too brusquely woken from
by screams in an unfamiliar tongue
over pounding drums that are not our own.

★

I touch my wife under the swansdown coverlet
with the bewildered lasciviousness of a young groom.
Grizzled from too many pointless campaigns,
I ache at times for the dull
doze of retirement, Virgil on tap,
some absurdly temperate ideal.
For the villa in the sun
under a sugary warmth of figs.
The pool with serving maids on the rim
at one's beck and call. Working on my memoirs.
Settling scores of long date.
Then burning them all
before it gets too late.

★

The wind keeps whistling its tussocky tune
through the long nights, like a relentless lunatic,
snuffing out rush-lights and hope,
right up against sleep,
slightly briny from the wave-tops
of bottomless, faraway lochs,
their black waters scored by tribal boats
whose masts rattle with suspended skulls,
each coracle's tarred hull
in league with long-necked aquatic monsters
a hands-breadth-deep beneath them.
We have it direct from the natives
in first-hand intelligence reports
before we blind them, clamp their tongues
in our blacksmith's tongs fresh from the forge
and squeeze tight
till something gives.

★

From the 9th Batavian Cohort, from Flavius
Cerialis, prefect: from us to them.
From the wild wastes of the north by mule
to the echoing marble halls
striped with sunshine, fog off the Tiber
draping the docks and barges, the outstretched hands
of the painted dignitaries in marble,
all the saving paraphernalia of the Empire.
Parcel after parcel. From my hunting-nets
to her ceramic bowls coddled in cloth rags
unwound to the fragrance of heat and dust,
of journeys longed for,
plodded from the deserts of Syria.
Wagonloads of slender amphorae:
Spanish oil, fine black pepper from India,

fish sauces from Portugal. The world
is at our beck and call: we are cared for
from frontier to frontier.
Beyond that line
is doubt and mistrust, beyond the buffer zone
lie the incantatory, slippery realms
where even our agents – even the feathered,
full-blooded indigenes – won't go
without a preliminary fuss. A zone
where death can be slow: the barbarians'
only artform. Look, admit it.
They have no culture.

★

Some maintain, of course,
that there is nothing out there at all.
Until it stirs. Until the solitary gorse
creeps forward, so slowly over days
it is undetected by even the alertest
of my sentries. Behind the crenellations
we are a shifting of shadows
to them. Spectres. Ghosts
above the slope. Poisonous berries
in our water supply! My principal nightmare.
You see it? To the left of that stretch
of bright bog-moss below the scree
(*Keep your head down*, as some naïve cretin
is said to have said to the visiting Emperor
in our grandparents' time).
The one shaped like a leopard,
or a wolf, or like anything
it pleases you to see.

Now tap the slab we're leaning on.
This is far more real than you or me.

★

'Heatherwards', as my captain says,
pointing his cavalry sword
slender as an icicle. Another recce.
I like his humour.
Verve, and doing what you're told:
all a soldier needs. Doing
what you're told and verve.
An uneasy equilibrium. I'm no
philosopher, but it seems to me
that muscle is just as important.
Public safety depends upon it.
Useful as pork fat,
sour wine, a hundred pounds of sinew.
As blood on the sacrificial stone.
Some of my men, for instance,
are huge, their arms like the articulated
limbs of insects, or moulded armour:
the shoulders sit on the biceps
like packs, like something separate,
hard as stone, undentable until an axe
of Pictish iron swoops,
devastating all that miracle,
its harmony of verve and obedience.

★

The medical orderlies
yelling for assistance, yesterday.
Tendons hanging like rope
from my best man, Tertius the Bear,
his huge torso soaked, up-splattered on his jaw.
Ambush. A patrol gone wrong.
My feeling, to be honest,
among the shouts and curses, the pointless
scurryings about, the Bear's ghastly shudders:
we are the ones interned.
Not just us, but the entire Empire
a sprawling, well-guarded camp
from frontier to frontier,
from wet heather to scorching sand.
The gods bored with the whole thing
and already on the wing.

★

Enough of that. Here,
a cup of Massic wine.
Good health. The flicker of firelight
in loving eyes. Oysters tasting of the sacred Thames.
The numberless units of enemy cavalry
are so much chaff to these.
Blow them away, my dearest one.

★

The roads are still as bad.

ACKNOWLEDGEMENTS

Agincourt was commissioned by BBC Radio 3's *Sunday Feature* (first broadcast 25 October 2015), while *The Monster* was commissioned by the Bristol Festival of Ideas in 2016. *Conference* was requested by the British Council, Cologne.

With thanks to the *London Review of Books* and *PN Review* where some of these poems first appeared.